D0435167

sleepover Girls crafts

Spa PROJECTS
You Can Make and Share

by Mari Bolte
illustrated by Paula Franco

CAPSTONE PRESS
a capstone imprint

Table of CONTENTS

Pack your bags for fun with the Sleepover Girls! Every Friday, Maren, Ashley, Delaney, and Willow get together for crafts, fashion, cooking, and, of course, girl talk! Read the books, get to know the girls, and dive in to this book of cool projects that are Sleepover Girl staples!

Create glittery bath bombs that sparkle and shine, or paint your nails with star-studded style. Make lotion bars that fit your Sleepover Girl personality, and moisturize with a face mask perfect for any chocoholic. Choose your favorite scents, phone some friends, and start pampering with your very own Sleepover Girls.

Willow Marie Keys

Patient and kind, Willow is a wonderful confidante and friend. (Just ask her twin, Winston!) She is also a budding artist with creativity for miles. Willow's Bohemian style suits her flower child within.

Maren Melissa Taylor

Maren is what you'd call "personality-plus"— sassy, bursting with energy, and always ready with a sharp one-liner. You'll often catch Maren wearing a hoodie over a sports tee and jeans. An only child, Maren has adopted her friends as sisters.

Ashley Francesca Maggio

Ashley is the baby of a lively Italian family. This fashionista-turned-blogger is on top of every style trend via her blog, Magstar. Vivacious and mischievous, Ashley is rarely sighted without her beloved "purse puppy," Coco.

Delaney Ann Brand

Delaney's smart, motivated, and always on the go! You'll usually spot low-maintenance Delaney in a ponytail and jeans (and don't forget her special charm bracelet, with charms to symbolize her Sleepover Girl buddies.)

Sleepover Sugar

The Sleepover Girls were a little unsure about Ashley's new friend, Sophie. But Sophie knew the best way to win over the Sleepover Girls was with sweet-smelling sugar scrub! A few simple ingredients mean DIYing these scrubbing cubes has never been easier.

WHAT YOU'LL NEED

cheese grater

1 bar unscented soap

¼ cup (60 milliliters) coconut oil

3–4 drops vanilla essential oil

¼ cup (60 mL) coffee grounds

1 cup (240 mL) white sugar

ice cube tray or sugar cube mold

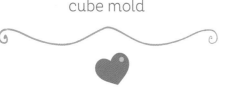

1
Use a cheese grater to grate soap until you have ½ cup (120 mL).

2
Combine the soap and coconut oil in a bowl. Microwave on high for 10 seconds. Remove and stir. Repeat until the soap and oil are melted, and stir until combined.

3
Stir in vanilla essential oil.

4
Stir in coffee grounds and sugar.

5
Quickly press sugar mixture into mold or ice cube tray.

6
Freeze mold for 30 minutes. Then remove sugar cubes. You can cut them to a smaller size, if desired. Store in an airtight container. To use, rub them on your skin to exfoliate in the shower. Rinse well.

Cocoa Glow

Bond with your besties and get pampered at the same time! This nourishing mask tastes as good as it smells. Mix it up and get moisturizing.

WHAT YOU'LL NEED

1/3 cup (80 mL) cocoa powder

¼ cup (60 mL) honey

2 tablespoons (30 mL) Greek yogurt

squeeze of lemon juice

1 Mix all ingredients with a whisk or in a blender. Blend until smooth. The mask mixture can be stored in the refrigerator for up to three days.

2 To use, wash your face well. Use a gentle exfoliant to scrub away any dead skin.

3 Apply face mask. Leave on for 20 minutes.

4 Rinse with warm water.

TIP:
To add a soothing element to your face mask, add 2 to 3 tablespoons (30 to 45 mL) of powdered oatmeal. (Just pulse dry oatmeal in a blender until it becomes a powder.)

TIPS:
To make an extra moisturizing mask, add half a mashed avocado or a drizzle of olive oil.

For a fruity twist, add three strawberries or some mashed banana.

Charm Bars

Nothing makes the ultimate favor like these lovely lotion bars. They can be colored, scented, and shaped to match your Sleepover Girl personality.

WHAT YOU'LL NEED

½ cup (120 mL) beeswax cubes or pellets

½ cup (120 mL) coconut oil

½ cup (120 mL) almond oil

skin-safe fragrance oil or essential oil (optional)

soap colorants, such as mica powder or jojoba beads (optional)

shaped mold

1 Melt beeswax, coconut oil, and almond oil in a microwave-safe bowl for 30 seconds. Stir. Repeat until everything is completely melted and combined.

2 Add fragrance and color, if desired.

3 Pour mixture into a liquid measuring cup, to make pouring easier.

4 Pour mixture into mold. Leave at room temperature for several hours, or overnight, until set. If you're in a hurry, you can place the mold in the freezer.

TIP:
Beeswax can be found at craft and health stores. Coconut and almond oil can be found in the baking or personal care aisles of your grocery store.

Sandwich Style

Changing up your style has never been easier. With a bit of fabric and a sandwich bag, your spa accessories will be as stylish as you. Bring it along on your next sleepover. Your BFFs will be begging for one too!

WHAT YOU'LL NEED

fabric measuring about 30 inches by 15 inches (76 by 38 centimenters)

double-sided tape

zip-top sandwich bag

Velcro strips

needle and thread or fabric glue

button

1 Lay the fabric flat on your work surface. Center the sandwich bag on the fabric. Fold over each edge of the fabric twice for clean seams. Use double-sided tape to stick the fabric to the sandwich bag.

2 Fold the long sides of the fabric around the sandwich bag. Stick the fabric to the bag with double-sided tape.

3 Fold the bottom of the fabric up. The bottom should reach about three-quarters of the way from the top of the bag. Use tape to stick the fabric to the sandwich bag.

4 Fold down the top of the fabric. The seam of the top should be even with the top of the sandwich bag.

5 Use Velcro strips on the inside of the top flap and the front of the bag to keep the flap closed.

6 Sew or use glue to add a button to the outside of the top flap.

Glitter Bombs

Willow thought dousing Winston with glitter was the best way to wake up her twin. These glitter bombs are a lot less messy and smell a lot better! They'll look (almost!) good enough to eat. Drop one in the bath and enjoy a soothing, fizzing, and moisturizing experience.

WHAT YOU'LL NEED

green tea

food coloring

½ cup (120 mL) baking soda

¼ cup (60 mL) corn starch

¼ cup (60 mL) colored bath salts
or Epsom salts

¼ cup (60 mL) citric acid

1 tablespoon (15 mL) coconut oil

tart molds

1 Follow the instructions on the tea bags to make a double-strong cup of tea. Add food coloring, and mix with a spoon until the tea is evenly colored. Set aside.

2 In a large bowl, combine the baking soda, corn starch, bath salts, and citric acid. Whisk to remove lumps.

3 Add coconut oil. Use your fingers to thoroughly mix in the oil. The mixture should have a crumbly texture when you're finished.

continued

4 Slowly add 1 tablespoon (15 mL) of the green tea to the mixture. Use your hands to mix well.

5 Add another ½ tablespoon (7.5 mL) of tea. Mix well. (Do not add too much or too fast, or the mixture will bubble and react.)

6 If you've added enough water, the mixture should hold together when you squeeze it. If there's not enough water, slowly add another ½ tablespoon.

7 Firmly press the mixture into a small cup, ramekin, or tart mold. Let dry while you make the frosting.

TIP:
You can find citric acid in the canning section of the supermarket. Health food stores and pharmacies also may carry citric acid. And, if all else fails, check online.

FOR THE FROSTING

WHAT YOU'LL NEED

3 tablespoons (45 mL) meringue powder

5-6 tablespoons (75-90 mL) green tea

¼ teaspoon (1.2 mL) cream of tartar

1 pound (455 grams) powdered sugar

frosting bag fitted with a jumbo tip

glitter and/or sprinkles

1 In a glass bowl, mix the meringue powder and tea. Add cream of tartar and powdered sugar. Use an electric mixer to beat on high for 7-8 minutes, until the frosting is thick and fluffy.

2 Spoon the frosting into a frosting bag.

3 Frost the cupcake bath bombs however you want. Decorate with glitter and sprinkles.

4 Let cupcake bath bombs dry overnight before removing from molds.

Hair Chalk

Ashley's colored locks didn't go as planned at Sophie's sleepover. Auburn Vixen? More like Orange Ogre! Get the color you really want with easy-to-change dye in a rainbow of hues.

WHAT YOU'LL NEED

water in a spray bottle
soft pastels
curling iron
hair spray

1 Spray the section of hair you want to color with water.

2 Using the long sides, rub a pastel onto hair. Be sure to color both the top and bottom of the hair.

3 Run the hot curling iron over the colored section. This will set the color.

4 Mist hair with hair spray.

5 Repeat with additional hair sections and colors.

TIP:
Wear an old shirt and disposable gloves to protect your hands and clothing.

Mad Hatter Cups

Help the Sleepover Girls get ready for Valley View's production of *Alice in Wonderland*. Join the dress rehearsal, and tell the plain pottery to "move down" for these Mad Hatter cups!

WHAT YOU'LL NEED

plain white teacup

rubbing alcohol

cotton swabs

black fine tip porcelain marker

porcelain paint

soft paintbrushes

paper plate

1 Clean the teacup with rubbing alcohol and cotton swabs. Wash your hands too.

2 Use the fine tip marker to draw your design. Be careful not to smear the ink. It should dry to the touch within 15 seconds.

3 Color in your design with porcelain paint and paintbrushes. Use the plate to mix colors, if desired.

4 Let teacup dry for at least 24 hours.

5 Place teacup directly on the oven rack in a cold oven. Set oven temperature to 300 degrees Fahrenheit (149 degrees Celsius). Let the teacup bake for 35 minutes.

6 Once time is up, turn off the oven. Allow teacup to cool completely inside the oven.

TIPS:
Porcelain paint can be thinned with water for a softer look.

Do not preheat the oven. Sudden changes in temperature may cause the cup to crack.

TIP:
If you make a mistake during painting, use a cotton swab and rubbing alcohol to quickly correct. If you decide you don't like your design after all, wash with soap and warm water or rub with alcohol. Then start over.

Fuzzy Warm Feet

Every sleepover hostess knows her guests' comfort is key. Help everyone relax with scented foot-warming slippers.

WHAT YOU'LL NEED

pencil

bedroom slippers

paper

scissors

flannel

pins

needle and thread

2 cups (480 mL) rice

scented oil

16-foot (1.8-meter)-long fluffy boa

hot glue and a glue gun

flower embellishment

FOR THE FOOT PADS

1 Trace the bottom of the slipper onto a piece of paper. Cut out.

2 Lay paper template over flannel. Trace and cut out two flannel pieces.

3 Flip paper template over. Trace and cut out two more flannel pieces. You should now have two top and two bottom piece.

4 Pin a top piece to a bottom piece. Sew together, leaving an end open. (See sewing instructions on page 25.) Repeat with the other foot insert. Set aside.

5 Pour rice into a zip-top bag. Add scented oil. (The scent will fade over time, so add more than you think is enough.) Seal and shake the bag to coat the rice.

6 Pour rice into the inserts. Sew foot inserts shut.

continued

FOR THE SLIPPERS

1 Cut the boa in half.

2 Apply a line of hot glue where the top of the slipper and the sole meet. Carefully press one end of the boa into the glue.

3 Curve the boa and continue gluing and pressing the next row. Make a zigzag pattern working toward the toe. Repeat with the other slipper.

4 Apply a small amount of hot glue to the back of the flower. Press flower onto the slipper and hold until set. Repeat with the other slipper.

5 When you're ready to use your slippers, heat inserts in the microwave for a minute. Then place an insert into each slipper.

SEWING BY HAND

Slide the thread through the eye of the needle. Tie the end of the thread into a knot. Poke the needle through the underside of the fabric. Pull the thread through the fabric to the knotted end. Poke your needle back through the fabric and up again to make a stitch.

Continue weaving the needle in and out of the fabric, making small stitches in a straight line. When you are finished sewing, make a loose stitch. Thread the needle through the loop and pull tight. Cut off remaining thread.

Magstar Mani

Ashley puts the "Ash" in fashion with her blog, Magstar. Give it the "thumbs up" with star-studded nails. Who knows? Maybe your mani will get its own blog feature—"Nailed It!"

WHAT YOU'LL NEED

clear tape, in a dispenser

teal nail polish

star-shaped hole punch

silver polish

tweezers

clear nail polish

pink nail art pen

1. Paint clear tape with at least three coats of teal polish. Let polish dry before applying the next coat.

2. When polish is completely dry, use hole punch to punch out a star shape.

3. Paint all nails with silver polish. Do not let dry.

4. Use tweezers to lift and press a star shape into the center of your index finger. Let polish dry.

5. Paint nails with clear polish. Let dry.

6. Use nail art pen to draw an M shape over the star. Add dots to the rest of your nails for decoration, if desired. Let dry.

7. Seal design with a topcoat of clear polish. Let dry completely.

Polish Phones

To reach max relaxation, you can't skip soothing tunes. Get the most out of your playlist by giving your headphones the spa treatment. Luke Lewis' "Coming Home" has never sounded sweeter.

WHAT YOU'LL NEED

earbud headphones
alligator clip
nail polish in two colors
glitter nail polish
clear topcoat nail polish

1   If using old earbuds, clean gently with soap and warm water before painting.

2   Use alligator clip to clip headphones to a solid surface, such as a table.

3   Paint the headphone cord completely with matte nail polish. Let dry completely. Add a second coat, if desired.

4   Paint the headphone cord completely with glitter nail polish. Let dry completely.

5   Use the second colored nail polish to make evenly spaced dots along the cord. Let dry completely.

6   Use a single color of polish on any connecting areas or ports.

7   Cover all painted areas with clear polish. Let dry completely.

TIP:
Do not paint anything metal or anything that goes in your ears. Also avoid painting over any holes, as this will distort your headphones' sound.

Spa Sundaes

Sweets aren't just for your stomach. Send your friends home with their own salon-in-a-cup. Scoop spa favorites and sprinkle with your sundae best for a tasty, tootsie-friendly treat.

WHAT YOU'LL NEED

fuzzy spa socks

sample-sized beauty items, such as lip balms, hand sanitizers, nail polishes, small emery boards, scrubs, or lotion bars

sundae glasses

ribbon

emery board

loofah

comb

red bath bead

1 Tuck one sock inside the other.

2 Fill socks halfway with beauty items. Fold sock to close.

3 Place socks in sundae glasses. Top with loofah.

4 Tie a ribbon around the sundae glasses. Add emery board and comb.

5 Top spa sundae with bath bead.

Read More

Doherty, Tricia. *Locker Looks and Study Nooks: A Crafting and Idea Book for a Smart Girl's Guide: Middle School.* American Girl. Middleton, Wisc.: American Girl, 2014.

Kenney, Karen Latchana. *Cool Slumber Parties: Perfect Party Planning for Kids.* Minneapolis: ABDO Pub., 2012.

Mattel. *Ever After High: Sleepover Spellebration Party Planner.* Ever After High. New York: Little, Brown and Co., 2014.

Snap Books are published by Capstone, 1710 Roe Crest Drive, North Mankato, Minnesota 56003.

www.capstonepub.com

Library of Congress Cataloging-in-Publication Data
Bolte, Mari., author.
Spa projects you can make and share / by Mari Bolte
illustrated by Paula Franco.
pages cm. — (Snap. Sleepover girls crafts)
Summary: "Step-by-step instructions teach readers how to create spa products at home, including bath bombs, lotion bars, and other aromatherapy items"— Provided by publisher.

ISBN 978-1-4914-1736-2 (library binding)
ISBN 978-1-4914-1741-6 (eBook PDF)

1. Handicraft—Juvenile literature. 2. Hygiene products—Juvenile literature. I. Franco, Paula, illustrator. II. Title.

TP983.B655 2015

745.593—dc23   2014012717

Designer: Tracy Davies McCabe
Craft Project Creator: Kim Braun
Photo Stylist: Sarah Schuette
Art Director: Nathan Gassman
Production Specialist: Laura Manthe

Photo Credits:
All Photos By Capstone Press:
Karon Dubke

Artistic Effects:
Shutterstock

Printed in the United States of America in North Mankato, Minnesota.
032014   008087CGF14